EXPLORE THE U.S.A.

CALIFORNIA

Karen Durrie

LET'S READ
AV2 BY WEIGL
ADDED VALUE · AUDIO VISUAL

www.av2books.com

LET'S READ

AV²
BY WEIGL™

ADDED VALUE • AUDIO VISUAL

AV² provides enriched content that supplements and complements this book. Weigl's AV² books strive to create inspired learning and engage young minds in a total learning experience.

Your AV² Media Enhanced books come alive with...

Audio
Listen to sections of the book read aloud.

Video
Watch informative video clips.

Embedded Weblinks
Gain additional information for research.

Try This!
Complete activities and hands-on experiments.

Key Words
Study vocabulary, and complete a matching word activity.

Quizzes
Test your knowledge.

Slide Show
View images and captions, and prepare a presentation.

... and much, much more!

Go to **www.av2books.com**, and enter this book's unique code.

BOOK CODE

V381427

AV² by Weigl brings you media enhanced books that support active learning.

Published by AV² by Weigl
350 5th Avenue, 59th Floor
New York, NY 10118
Website: www.av2books.com   www.weigl.com

Library of Congress Cataloging-in-Publication Data

Durrie, Karen.
 California / Karen Durrie.
   p. cm. -- (Explore the U.S.A.)
 Audience: Grades K-3.
 Includes bibliographical references and index.
 ISBN 978-1-61913-329-7 (hbk. : alk. paper)
 1. California--Juvenile literature. I. Title.
 F861.3.D87 2012
 979.4--dc23
                    2012014756

Printed in the United States of America in North Mankato, Minnesota
1 2 3 4 5 6 7 8 9   16 15 14 13 12

052012
WEP040512

Project Coordinator: Karen Durrie
Art Director: Terry Paulhus

Weigl acknowledges Getty Images as the primary image supplier for this title.

CALIFORNIA

Contents

2   AV^2 Book Code
4   Nickname
6   Location
8   History
10   Flower and Seal
12   Flag
14   Animal
16   Capital
18   Goods
20   Fun Things to Do
22   Facts
24   Key Words

This is California.
It is called the Golden State.
There is gold in California.

5

This is the shape of California. It is in the west part of the United States. California borders Oregon, Nevada, and Arizona.

Where is California?

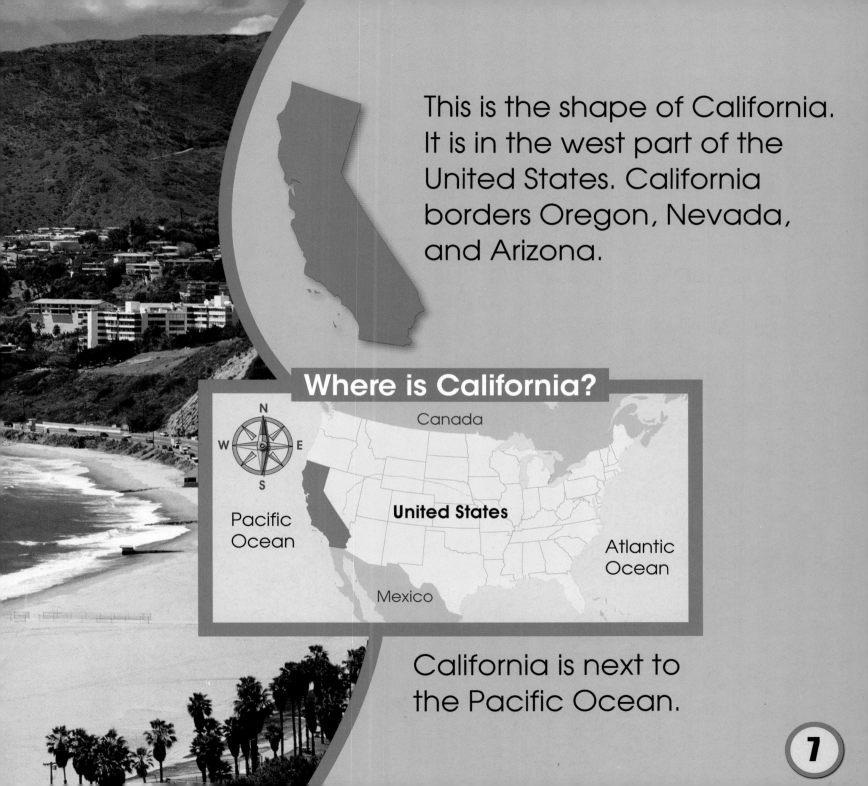

Canada

N
W E
S

Pacific Ocean

United States

Atlantic Ocean

Mexico

California is next to the Pacific Ocean.

Gold was found in California in 1848. People from all over the world came to look for gold. This was called the Gold Rush.

The biggest gold nugget found in California weighed 195 pounds.

9

The California poppy is the state flower. It can be yellow or orange. American Indians used poppies for food.

The state seal has a goddess, a man, and four ships.

The man on the state seal is a miner.

This is the state flag of California. It has a grizzly bear and a red star.

The bear on the flag stands for strength.

13

The state animal of California is the grizzly bear. California once had about 10,000 grizzly bears.

Today, there are no California grizzly bears.

15

This is the capital city of California. It is named Sacramento. Sacramento has been the state capital since 1854.

Sacramento has the biggest railroad museum in North America.

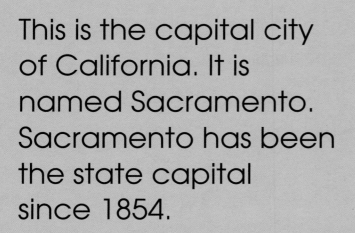

Grapes grow in California. They can be green, red, black, blue, purple, or gold. Grapes can be used to make juice.

More than 30,000 tons of grapes are grown in California each year.

California has the tallest trees on Earth. These trees can grow up to 378 feet tall.

People visit state parks to see the giant trees.

CALIFORNIA FACTS

These pages provide detailed information that expands on the interesting facts found in the book. These pages are intended to be used by adults as a learning support to help young readers round out their knowledge of each state in the *Explore the U.S.A.* series.

Pages 4–5

California is called the Golden State. This nickname comes from the discovery of gold in California in 1848, setting off the California Gold Rush. Gold production hit an all-time high of $81 million in 1852. The fields of golden poppies seen each spring in California also make the state's nickname appropriate.

Pages 6–7

On September 9, 1850, California became the 31st state to join the United States. California is on the West Coast and is bordered by Oregon, Nevada, and Arizona. It is the third largest state and is 800 miles (1,287 kilometers) long. The Sierra Nevada mountain range lies on the eastern border of California.

Pages 8–9

James Marshall found gold nuggets in Coloma, California, in 1848. In March of that year, a California newspaper announced Marshall's discovery. More people soon found gold deposits. As news spread, people began migrating to California to find gold. More than 300,000 people came to California during the Gold Rush, which ended in 1864.

Pages 10–11

Poppies are found throughout California. California poppies are also nicknamed the flame flower and the cup of gold. The state celebrates Poppy Day on April 6 each year. The state seal shows the industries of California. The grapes represent the agriculture of the state. The seal also has the word "Eureka" on it. *Eureka* is a Greek word that means "I have found it." This refers to the discovery of gold in California.

Pages 12–13

The California flag was designed in 1846 by revolutionaries fighting for independence from Mexico. At that time, California was part of Mexico. It was called Alta California. The red star represents an earlier flag called the 1836 California Lone Star flag. It was white with a red star in the middle.

Pages 14–15

The grizzly bear was chosen as the state animal in 1953. These animals were once the largest predators in California. Settlers began encroaching on grizzly bear habitat. When bears began attacking livestock, settlers began to hunt the bears. The last California grizzly bear was killed in 1922.

Pages 16–17

Located in central California, Sacramento became the state capital in 1854. The city has a famous historic district. Old Sacramento is a 28-acre (11-hectare) state park with historic landmarks and museums. The California State Railroad Museum features 21 restored locomotives and train cars. Over half a million people visit the museum each year.

Pages 18–19

California is often called the Grape State because of its productive grape industry. Much of the state has a Mediterranean climate, which is ideal for growing grapes. Ninety-eight percent of the grapes eaten in the United States come from California. More than 9,000 farmers work on grape farms in the state.

Pages 20–21

Sequoias and redwoods grow throughout California. Sequoia trees are some of the tallest trees in the world. The largest living tree can be found in Sequoia National Park, near Three Rivers, California. The tree is 102 feet (31 meters) in circumference. The California redwood is the official state tree. One of the tallest redwoods in the world is more than 379 feet (116 m) tall. It stands in a remote California forest.

KEY WORDS

Research has shown that as much as 65 percent of all written material published in English is made up of 300 words. These 300 words cannot be taught using pictures or learned by sounding them out. They must be recognized by sight. This book contains 55 common sight words to help young readers improve their reading fluency and comprehension. This book also teaches young readers several important content words, such as proper nouns. These words are paired with pictures to aid in learning and improve understanding.

Page	Sight Words First Appearance
4	in, is, it, state, the, there, this
7	and, next, of, part, to, where
8	all, came, for, found, from, look, over, people, was, world
11	a, American, be, can, food, has, Indian, man, on, or, used
15	about, animal, are, had, no, once
16	been, city, named
19	each, grow, make, than, they, year
20	Earth, feet, see, these, trees, up

Page	Content Words First Appearance
4	California, gold
7	Arizona, Nevada, Oregon, Pacific Ocean, shape, United States
8	Gold Rush, nugget, pounds
11	flower, goddess, miner, poppy, seal, ships
12	bear, flag, grizzly bear, star, strength
16	capital, museum, North America, Sacramento
19	grapes, juice, tons
20	parks

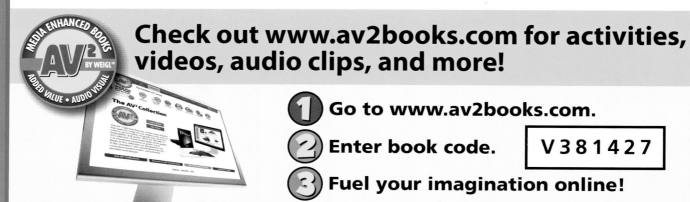